Steller's Jay Blue Sway

**Photos and Poems by
Dwayne Cole**

Parson's Porch Books

Steller's Jay Blue Sway: Photos and Poems
ISBN: Softcover 978-1-936912-92-8
Copyright © 2024 by Dwayne Cole

Parson's Porch Books is an imprint of Parson's Porch *&* Company (PP*&*C) in Cleveland, Tennessee. PP*&*C is a self-funded charity which earns money by publishing books of noted authors, representing all genres. Its face and voice is **David Russell Tullock** (dtullock@parsonsporch.com).

Parson's Porch *&* Company *turns books into bread & milk* by sharing its profits with the poor.

www.parsonsporch.com

This Photo is by Donna Dewhurst.

Dedication

This book is dedicated to Scott Lawrence and Donna Dewhurst, our friends and good neighbors. Isn't it delightful to have nature loving friends nearby? You can see Donna's skill as a nature photographer in this photo and in her profile photos on Facebook.

(All other bird photos in this book are mine, and were taken over the last decade in Anchorage, Alaska.)

Preface

When words become unclear, I shall focus with photographs. —Ansel Adams

Value of Contemplating in Nature

The central purpose of my poetry is to become one with the beauty and wonder of nature. In the eyes of the Steller's jay lighting in my hand for sunflower heart seeds, I see stars twinkling—I see a spinning universe. In that moment, I am participating in divine myth. I experience the gift of wonder.

We contemplate in nature in order
to understand our existence in the natural world.
We become a part of what we think about. In these moments we are actively becoming a part of nature. Participating not as object but as subject to subject.

This encounter with nature is for awakening a new self-understanding. Birds in myth have been symbolic of release from the earth.
In observing the heart birds, they become kin, friends, giving us wings. We see new possibilities of soaring with them in blue skies.

Heaven shines on me
Healing my broken spirit
Angels singing praise

I feed you heart seeds
Touch your heart and feel your soul
See world more clearly

Introduction

My wife, Beth, and I retired to Alaska in 2011, to become caregivers of grandchildren, as our daughter and son-in-law started their medical practice.

In that move, I became a photographer/poet. All the natural beauty and wonder of Alaska spoke to me saying, "Take my picture. Write a poem about me."

Alaska, the last wild frontier, is so beautiful, so very beautiful! I daily take pictures of Alpenglow sunrises and sunsets, and occasionally the Aurora Borealis. Glaciers, waterfalls, cascading streams, rivers and lakes are abundant in Alaska.

Moose and bears are an almost daily presence. Alaska has one moose for every four citizens, and one bear for every five. Both moose and bears have walked through automatic opening glass doors in seeking food.

My poetry speaks of the beauty and wonder, magical music of the spheres, coming on wings of inspiration.

This book, *Steller's Jay Blue Sway, is polysemantic nature poetry that is inspired by one of my favorite quotes from Einstein: "Look deep into nature, and then you will understand everything better."*

In making this journey into nature—

No ticket is needed
Nature's not a place to just visit
It's home every day

Let's open our hearts
In compassion to each other
Let kindness blossom

In the heart bird's eyes
We see radiance of all things
An epiphany

Power of Bird Myth

Contemplating in nature is powerful, mythic even. Mythic bird poetry calls your soul out of its hiding place. Some of the bird poems in this book have factual origins, while others are fictional and somewhat humorous. But myths are more than mere stories and they serve a more profound purpose in ancient and modern cultures. Myths are more than true. Myths explain the world and our experience in the world. You can feel the power of myth, a feeling of discovery, making you want to take wings and soar in blue skies.

Mythic bird poems are songs of the universe singing our soul awake. When I feed the birds,

I dance to the music of the spheres.

I wake to the music of angels singing.

The birds that come to my deck
are my brothers and sisters: we are kin.
One family drinking from the same stream of life.

Dance with Steller's jays
Let their rhythm set your soul free
Myth of the ages

Bird myth calls us to think
To dream new possibilities
Dare to be different

A sudden gust of wind
Causes the tree leaves to whisper
Like the song of birds

How To Use This Book

Many of the photos and poems in this book were shared with our grandchildren from the time they started to kindergarten in 2011, and until they finished high school. We wanted to create a love for nature poetry and the beauty of birds. If you wish to accomplish this wonder in your life and share it with others, the suggestions below will be helpful.

1. It is hard to look at the pictures and poems without feeling joy and happiness. Take time for this; and if children are involved, let them express their happiness. You might turn some of the photos into a game of I spy. Do you see what I see?

2. One of the purposes of this book is to teach kindness toward all living things, and especially toward all children. Ask how we can show kindness. (See my book, *Kindness Is Every Step*).

3. Use this book, *Steller's Jay Blue* Sway, as inspiration for learning proper use of cameras and photo techniques.

4. If you are sharing the book with children or youth, you might want to teach color pencil drawing of birds and nature scenes. Our grandchildren loved this activity. As they get older you can move to watercolors and oil painting.

God cares for the birds
and God cares for you.

D. Cole

This is one of the early color pencil drawings
I did with our grandchildren.

5. My wife, Beth, and I wanted to teach children to write nature poems. Many of the poems in this book are haiku. Haiku has been seen as a good way to start learning and teaching poetry. Sijo is the logical next step in this poetic adventure.

6. My books, *Heart Haiku: Alaska Inspired Photos and Poems;* and *Heart Sijo: Alaska Inspired Photos and Poems,* will be helpful in understanding and teaching these forms of poetry. These books can be purchased online from Parsons Porch Books, Amazon, and Barnes & Noble.

7. Let your love of children guide you in finding other creative ways to use this book. Send me your ideas, please.

From my dining room table,
I see a Steller's jay posing.

Sun breaks through dark clouds,
revealing Alpenglow colors.

Artist's palette wonder,
Mother Nature on display.

Hope is the thing with feathers
That perches in the soul,
And sings the tune without the words,
And never stops at all.

—Emily Dickinson

Steller's Jay Blue Sway
wins my heart every day.
Dances my blues away.
Links me to faith, hope, and love.
Eternity is now!

In all four seasons
Steller's jays visit me
They hold sway for sure

Blue Preacher's Cape

God cares for the birds,
and God cares for you and me.
—See Matthew 6:26

Steller's jay with raised nape
Dressed in dark blue preacher's cape
Perched on communion rail
Balancing with light blue tail

Piercing eyes send a shudder
through many souls
Whether good or evil is born
The gods blush and demons quake

When he spies me
Sitting in my Cracker Barrel rocker
He nods as if waiting for
An amen shocker

Or maybe since he looked tipsy
From too much communion wine
Calling me an unrepeatable name

Part II

Chatter at the Altar---

Steller's jays have a kinship with preachers
Know God a lot better
Jays see God's face shining in the morning
And live joyfully all the day

Prophets not allowed to see God's face
Eyes of wrath sometimes best avoided
Both jays and preachers chatter a lot
Give the altar call while prancing

Jays store no money in the bank
Often fly on a half tank
Know God cares for the birds
No need to worry

Birds trust the sunset to move to sunrise
Reaching out with warmth
Each celestial day
For this is nature's way

Some preachers
in their prayerful moments have learned
love is more than chatter
at the altar table

Smartest of the birds
I will make the winning mark
So can all of you

Have no iPad
Nature is my sketch pad
My antics will pencil

A message so sweet
Just listen to my tweets
Sing alleluia

Power of bird myth
Myth combines intelligence and wit
Songs of all ages
Bird Songs of universe
Dancing my blues away

Steller's jays visit me
in Anchorage year-round for peanuts
Antics inspire poems

Friendship Sonnet

Steller's jays need loving heart friends,

joyfully caring for one another.

In social isolation, I need friends.

Friends to play and sing together.

When the tips of our fingers touch,

eyes shine with compassion.

Cost of peanuts is not too much.

Can't measure the value of passion.

Crowds are sometimes very fickle.

Mob violence is for real, and

not worth even a plugged nickel.

Jesus paid the price on the cross.

We can count everything else as loss.

What a caring Friend we have in Jesus.

Classical Notes

All the beautiful notes
classical musicians use are already here
in nature's bird songs.

Even the rapper's rhythms
can be felt in the morning's prelude
of the Steller's jay cadences.

In the evolutionary process
we are all kin, we are all one.

(In his book, *Born to Sing*, Charles
Hartshorne makes these musical claims after
years of studying bird songs.)

Smartest of the birds.
I will write this message:
Life is precious!

(If we could live and teach this truth
to our children, it would change the world.)

In myth, birds sing our soul awake.

Spring Has Arrived

Spring has arrived on wings
of inspiration and hope.

Yet the snow is so very deep:
the heart birds are asking for treats.

If I can save one bird from pain,
I shall count it as gain.

Hearts beating fast
Angel wings spread in gratitude
Could be a valentine

Eye to eye contact
Hand to hand friendship for real
Zestful adventure

Steller's jay antics.
I will perform for peanuts—
Add peanuts to grocery list.

Are the morning kisses the sweetest?

(A sand dab poem by Mary Oliver, named after the sand dab fish. It is often just one line, like this one.)

Steller's jays are bonding
Soon be spring mating time

Wouldn't you love to know
what they are thinking

An evolutionary treasure
Kisses are forever

We are one with birds
Both have bodily sense organs
Feeling world as one

(Steller's jays mate for life. Both build the nest.
Incubate 3-5 eggs each breeding season, and both
feed the fledglings,)

Steller's jay miracle

Flies away with my heart

Love is in the air

Dwayne Cole

Blue sway dancing
Hops in to save my day
Joy is abounding

Steller's Jay Limerick

Once there was a Steller's jay
That came to my deck to play
Grandchildren dance with joy
It was like a windup toy
Oh what a happy delightful day

(See Glossary, pages 103-104 for definition of
limerick and other types of poems used in this book.)

Steller's jay antics

Performing for peanuts

Acts of great joy

(Be sure to wash hands before and after feeding
from your hands. Also wash seed containers and
feeders regularly).

Playing hide and seek

A child's spirit is hiding in us

Let us leap for joy

Art imitates life.

Life imitates art.

Clap your hands in joy
Bird antics sing our soul awake
Dance to the music

Cabin Fever Isolation Saga

For fun with grandchildren, I put this straw duck on my deck rail. Placed a peanut in its mouth and on the rail. A Steller's jay flew by and eye-balled it. Decided it was harmless, and landed on its back. Reached in and took peanut out of its mouth. Then it flew into cottonwood tree and ate it. I put another peanut in duck's mouth. Jay landed on rail in front of duck. Took peanut from its mouth again. This happened many times.

Flew home and told his kids,
I wondered where peanuts came from?
Today, I learned!

(This poem is a haibun: a prose statement followed by a haiku).

Attired in blue.
It's Steller's jay party time.
Let's dance and sing!

Myth about Steller's jay—
Fearless messenger of hope.
Brings good news.

Times of pandemic require furious dancing.

(Inspired by, *Hard Times Require Furious Dancing,*
Alice Walker).

My year-round friend
who eats peanuts from my hand—
Looking very pleased.
Came skiing in on deck rail.
Steller's jay antics amaze!

Steller's jay's eyes

Reflecting ancient star light

Illumine my soul

Saving a day from despair

Life is full of adventure

Steller's jay is fashioned like a galaxy.
Eyes are like small solar systems.

Music from the heavenly sphere.
Feathers as blue as deep azure sea.

Mother Nature waves a magic wand.
An evolutionary treasure takes wings.

Have a new camera
Nice rotating lens
It's named a Steller's Jay
Smartest of cameras

On camera tripod
Steller's jay sits begging
Where are the peanuts

Am I photographing Steller's jays? Or—
Are they photographing me?

Steller's jays are inquisitive.
Their eyes are always prying.

Once you feed them peanuts,
they will look for them every day.

God cares for the birds of the air,
and God cares for you and me.

Suffering ill effects from COVID shot. I was off kilter yesterday, but totally back to normal today. I am back to my photos and poems. Pulled up this photo and wrote haibun poem:

> My day changed when
> Steller's jay hopped on deck rail.
> Gave me a sideway glance.
> Never said a word, but
> Pictures flashed in my mind.
> This is message I heard—
> Smile, life is so beautiful.
> Full of wonder and love.
>
> The fates that haunt us
> Could not will our love away
> Our souls are dancing

From my rocking chair
I witness a Steller's jay
Pounce on a nuthatch

This flash of vibrant blue was different—A moment of horror even. I could not believe my eyes. A jay pounced on a little red-breasted nuthatch, one of my most loved birds—A beauty of nature that daily sings my heart awake. With nuthatch firmly held in his claws, he flew to a tree. Started pecking its eyes out. Feathers flew about as the jay devoured flesh. Now the family of four nuthatches that visited me, is down to three.

I knew Steller's jays were carnivorous, but witnessing the action was so painful. I resolved: No more peanuts from my hand today. There are enough spirit eaters in our world, without one living on my deck. I will still be kinder than necessary.

Flower petals fall
Flash of Steller's jay
Nuthatch feathers fly

Nature's Darkness

As a Whitehead process philosopher
and Jungian therapist, I look for meaning
and purpose of life. Nature is my lab.
In nature I see both good and evil, light and dark.

I see my friends, the Steller's jays,
displaying both rhythmic beauty of heaven's angels
dancing; and vicious denizens of hell robbing the
nest of little songbirds and eating the nestlings.
As a Christian minister I had to deal with this
mystery of life for fifty years. I will never forget
counseling one family whose son was killed
in the Viet Nam war. As we sat weeping together in
their back yard, the mother said,
"I can not find it in my heart to hate."

A few years later
I visit the Viet Nam Memorial Wall.
I walk by 58,307 names,
not a one the same.

Pause before one gray etching on
the Memorial Wall, a name from my past,
and remember—

Sitting in a backyard
caressing a mother's
sorrow and pain.

I remember—

Leaning in my preacher's robe
over a tear stained Bible.
Sharing words of kindness
with a Church family.

Offering embracing arms of
consoling love for a mother
whose hands seem to be stroking
a small child's cheeks.

Son came home from war—
In a wooden box.
Without his knitted socks.

It is hard not to hate our enemies,
especially as the conflicts grow more brutal.
The Israel/Hamas war in Gaza is atrocious.
Hell is empty of demons.
They have all taken up residence in Gaza.

While sitting on my deck, feeling the pain
of over 34,000 killed in Gaza by April 8, 2024,
with 70 percent being mothers and children—

A blue flash struck like a lightning bolt, claws
grabbed a nuthatch and flew to sliver birch tree.
The Steller's jay began to peck the eyes out
of the little bird. Red breast feathers floated to
ground. Tears flowed down my cheeks.

A flash from blue sky
Red breast feathers dripping blood
A tear fell from my eye

Theater of beauty
Turning into jaws of hell
Church bells are ringing

Life

Oh

AUM

Coming into being

Mortal

Silence

Immortal

Oh

AUM

("AUM chanting" is an ancient practice in Hinduism and Buddhism. It is a powerful way to connect us to the universe and our inner being. The sound of "AUM" is believed to be a universal sound. It's

like the sound of everything in the universe combined into one single note. I wrote this poem after reading *The Power of Myth: Joseph Campbell with Bill Moyers,* edited by Betty Sue Flowers.)

After **Nature's Darkness**

We need a moment of Alpenglow
Candy cane mountains
Taste and relish nature's gift
Let your soul be refreshed

There is nothing more cleansing
and renewing of sagging spirit than sitting
quietly, with Alpenglow sunrises and *Steller's Jay Blue Sway*. In these contemplative
moments I bring my feelings of despair and
radiant hope. Above all, I hear the call for
healing ecology.

Steller's Jay Haibun

Steller's jay comes to sliding glass door
to my deck and pecks on it. He waits
for me to come with a handful of peanuts.
I hold my hand out, he flies up,
lands on my finger tips,
and takes a peanut.
Then flies into the trees to eat,
and sometimes hide the nuts.
Then he's back for more.
Camera is on tripod,
and I snap pictures with a
remote clicker in my other hand.

Steller's jay magic
Universe spinning blue eyes
My spirit soars

(A haibun is a Japanese formatted poem that
starts with prose and ends with a haiku.

For fuller definition of kinds of poetry in this book
see Glossary, pages 103-104)

On my deck rail

Steller's jay exultation

Welcomes the new day

Blue Haibun

Reaching out my hand, I saw a flash of a blue. A Steller's jay, one of the most loved of birds in Anchorage, Alaska. The image called to my memory, George Wilhelm Steller, an 18th-century German botanist, zoologist, physician, and explorer who pioneered Alaskan natural history.

Bearing Steller's name
A family of "blue sway" jays
Eating from my hand

Photos are poems without words.

Dance of Wonder

Watching Steller's jay playing
I feel an artistic sensation
of something beyond control,
as if Mother Nature waved a magic wand.

The creative moment is fresh and new.
I experience an aesthetic moment of novelty.
All nature seems to share in this beautiful
rhythmic moment of mystery and harmony.

This aesthetic moment of creativity gathers the
whole universe, the many, as one, in a dance of
becoming. I dance into a new day with novel
possibilities. I breathe a prayer that my
grandchildren will turn novel possibilities
that enrich society into actualities.

(At this time, I invite you to turn to the beauty and
kindness training exercise on page 89 and spend
sometime meditating on values that enrich our
lives and help us see beauty in all lives.)

Steller's Jay Magical Sijo

Finger tips tenderly touching,
hearts beating in rhythm as one.

All for the cost of a few peanuts,
held in caring hands.

Wash hands before and after feeding.
Wash feeders weekly with love.

I look at the blue sky
Through deep blue feathery eyes
Every shade is there
Bright radiant day dreaming skies
Dark stormy nightmare skies

Steller's Jay Blue Sway
Tweets territorial tunes
Chases my blues away
Dark Delta variant clouds
Rainbow radiant promises

(Look carefully at the rainbow photo taken by my
grandson. In our culturally divided society both the
rainbow and Steller's jays sing of radiant hope.)

A Steller's jay lights on my deck rail
and sings, "Come and play with me,
but be sure to bring peanuts
as a special treat for me."

Steller's jay antics.
Dancing and clapping with joy.
In praise of friendship.

Friendship Sonnet

Steller's jays need loving friends,
caring for one another.
In social isolation, I too need friends.
Friends to play and sing together.

When the tips of our fingers touch,
eyes shine with compassion.
Cost of peanuts not too much.
Can't measure the value of passion.

Crowds are sometimes fickle.
Mob violence is for real, and
not worth a plugged nickel.

Jesus paid the price on the cross.
Count everything else as loss.
What a Friend we have in Jesus.

Wings of Inspiration
Steller's jay enjoying peanuts—
Love is this wide!

Steller's Jay Blue Sway—
All in the spirit of play
Wins my heart today!

Steller's jay liftoff
Angels fanning their wings
Hearts beating as one
In nature we are all kin
Many in One, One in many

Having a fun day.
Playing with four Steller's jays.
Hooray! Hooray!
Tossing and catching peanuts.
Missed a few as you can see!

Steller's jay dining
They come to deck door and beg
Peanuts are favorite

Feathers spread just right
Love is the thing with feathers
Illumined by sunlight

Steller's jays waiting.
Where are the peanuts, my friend?
Sorry, I am out.
Disappointed, one moons me!
Peanuts added to grocery list.

Steller's jay beauty

A favorite in all four seasons

Hold sway for sure

Wings of Inspiration

The birds of Alaska are so beautiful,

so very beautiful. Steller's jays

Visit us even on dark snowy days.

They also love the sunflower heart seeds

I share with them. Sharing is reciprocal.

They lift wings of inspiration that lift me.

My soul takes wings, flies in blue skies!

Steller's jay lesson—
Gifts of joy come in sharing.
Lifting songs of praise!

Blue as sky
Right after dawn

Blue as deep
Deep indigo sea

Blue as paint
On artist's palette

Blue eyes
Wink at me!

Come on now, Steller's jay.

Don't frown so unappreciative.

Peanuts are on the way!

On a cold snowy day I pulled up
Two of my favorite Steller's jay photos
and wrote an acrostic—

Steller's Jay Acrostic

S. Scintillating beauty

T. Treasure of evolution

E. Envy of Steller

L. Lovely blue skies

L. Loved by all

E. Every day wonder

R. Rise up and sing

S. Smartest of birds

J. Joy of all bird watchers

A. Anthem of praise is due

Y. Yours truly, with love

Steller's jays visit me year round.

I had just put sunflower heart seeds
in my communion saucer for them,
when two landed on the rail
squawking with joyful delight.
I was just to the left of saucer of seeds.
One looked at me with appreciation.
Ate some sunflower seeds;
and draping her blue minister's stole
around her shoulders, flew away.

    Steller's jay in flight
    Feathers spread just right
    A bird lover's delight

Magic saucer fills
Every few hours with new seeds
I'll take it to nest
Never know till you try it
My namesake collects things

(This is a young Steller's jay
testing his abilities.)

Eyeing the saucer.

Not peanuts? Heart seeds will do.

Thank you, friend.

Bird Songs

Steller's jays visit me everyday
Singing non-linguistic music

I cannot remember a time in my life
When I did not love birds

On our farm I heard roosters crow in sunrise
Crows in pecan tree caw in sunset

I heard bluebird songs on window sill
Before I could say words or trill

After 84+ years of observation
My non-verbal experience tells me

Birds have some form
of subjective experience

Wouldn't you love to know
what Steller's jays are tweeting

Not pugilistic
Will not draw gun and shoot

Maybe artistic song duel
Just ringing dinner bell

If only humans
could do so well

(This poem, Bird Songs, comes after reading the
intriguing "Introduction to Robert Burrell" by
Patricia Adams Farmer.)

Dwayne Cole

In process philosophy panexperientialism" is the idea that everything from humans down to subatomic particles have some form of experience. In reference to birds, it means that birds feel and experience subjectively and are not simply biologically determined. I could only write the bird haiku below after weeks of social isolation!!!

Bird Haiku in Three Words

ornithology

panexperientialism

therapeutical

Tragic Beauty

Complicated Steller's jays—
    Colorful and
        clever.

And dare we say, Cruel!

Will strike like a bolt of lightning.
    Rob a song bird's nest.
        Eat the nestlings alive.

Evolution thrives on
    Survival of the fittest.

Ravens, strong among the corvids,

    will rob the nests
    of weaker corvids,
    even magpies and jays.

Steller's jay singing
Blessing before eating seeds
Calls me to sing praise

Song Duel

Wouldn't you love to know
what this Steller's jay is tweeting

Not pugilistic
Will not draw gun and shoot

Maybe artistic song duel
Just ringing dinner bell

If only humans
could do so well

Decked in Blue

Steller's jay flies to rail, raindrops
shimmering on blue iridescent tail.

Announces his presence without shame.
Looks to see if all are in the game.

Bows to me sitting in my rocker.
Nods as if waiting for amen shocker!

Classical Notes

All the beautiful notes the classical
musicians use are already here
in nature's bird songs.
Even the rapper's rhythms
can be felt in the morning's
prelude of the Steller jay's cadences.

In the evolutionary process
we are all kin, we are all one.

DwayneCole

Walking Together Sonnet

Come, let us walk under leaves golden
To no one for now be beholden.
Hug and kiss under sun lit clear skies.
Heart-felt love twinkling in our eyes.

Come, let us walk in nature's beauty.
Play with *Steller's Jay Blue Sway* cutie.
Inspired by dusting of blue skies.
Heart-felt love twinkling in star-lit eyes.

Can our frail bodies hold heaven's light?
Nature's awesome beauty so very bright!
Nature's wonder is the thing with feathers.

Come let us play and sing together.
Steller is the poet luring on tender days,
All with nature's approving golden rays.

BEAUTY AND KINDNESS TRAINING EXERCISE

Poetry of beauty and kindness expressed in *Steller's Jay Blue Sway* is relational. Life is about relationships from birth till death. Relational beauty and kindness come naturally in contemplating in nature, and flows in personal ways.

Emphasizing the relational aspects of beauty broadens the definition, moving toward kindness.

Mindfully setting aside times to meditate on how we can better show beauty and kindness can help us become more sensitive and responsive to others within our everyday circles and move to include all persons.

Find a quiet time each day to contemplate on what you desire for your family and yourself:

* To be safe and secure.

* To be happy and at peace.

* To have good health.

* To be free from fear.

* To have fun times for all in family.

* To see beauty in all people, animals, and all living things.

A Summary Vision of Beauty

My vision for the world is that it move toward beauty. Seeing beauty in nature is a step in that direction.

Beauty is the key for understanding the loving and generous heart beat of nature.

The inner nourishing of a kind spirit in every person is one of the most important needs in our world today.

Beauty in one's heart is felt by the universe.

Yet, I am painfully aware of the chasm between this vision and its ultimate expression in our world that is so culturally divided.

Visions may be expressed in gentle words: They are more powerful when expressed in tender actions.

Centered in beauty and kindness We can transform our world.

Steller's Jay Miracle

One reason for playing with Steller's jay beauties is
so the joy we see in them will become our joy, and
their beauty will become our beauty.

The sense of being

one with Steller's jay beauty

is Mother Nature's gift.

Steller's jay beauty is nature laughing with us,
while moving us toward harmony.

Poetic Importance of Feeling

In each visit of Steller's jays,
I feel the universe incarnating itself in beauty.
Eyes convey the spinning universe.
Becoming one with nature's beautiful birds is
an inter-connective activity that gives value to
all of nature and inspires poetic ecology—
Tenderly preserving and saving the only world
we have for our existence.

In Steller's jays I see a hunger for life, a
hunger to propagate, to live. This is nature
unfurling itself, revealing its wonders. In this
mirror of nature I see my life unfolding in
beauty and wonder. This oneness with nature
is wrapped in photos and poems. The result is
enlivenment and a deep sense of gratitude.

The dead of winter Writing,
Steller's Jay Blue Sway,
World soul is alive

Conclusion

I fed you heart seeds
Touched your heart and felt your soul
Saw world with clarity
My heart and soul were reborn
One heart seed at a time

True Friendship

I know a friendship that is true
Formed in the Chugach foothills
Where nature welcomes all

A contemplative feeds birds
that visit his deck daily
in all kinds of weather

In spite of seasons
that come and go
Love never fails

Faithful friendship formed
Hope sent through the air
Love sings compassion

Kindness is reciprocal
Hearts beat as one
Take wings and fly

On a snowy day
Sunflower heart seeds provide warmth
Friends care for one another

Birds are symbols of release of the spirit
from the bondage to the earth.
They teach us how to fly in blue skies.

Steller's jays
Sing the music of my soul
Music of the spheres

Lessons Learned from Caring for Birds

1. Seeing our oneness with the universe. We are all kin, related as one.

2. Kindness is reciprocal healing.

3. Being kind to birds is as important to children as it is to birds.

4. Caring for birds brings joy to all.

5. Bird watching inspires hope.

6. Gives birth to creativity.

7. Teaches poetry. Photos are poems/poems are photos. Birds are poems.

8. Learn the importance of thanksgiving.

9. Become more grateful.

10. Bird watching instills beauty, wonder, goodness, art, novelty, and adventure.

11. Seeing value in nature leads to seeing value in our lives and value in all people.

12. Learning that life is precious. This lesson alone would change our world for the good.

13. Instills ecological concerns, saving our world for future generations.

14. Caring for birds nurtures the soul, leading to an inclusive love of all humankind. Learning this lesson reduces violence in our world.

15. Contemplating in nature is not evading the contemporary problems of life. It is preparing our soul to go into the world to effect positive change.

16. Caring for birds nurtures the experience of being alive—

The song of the universe.

Kindness Sonnet

Jesus, friend of the birds of the air,
only you understand my daily needs.
In my weakness I count it a blessing
that only you know my everyday deeds.

My collective unconscious is dark.
My shadow thoughts are tearing me apart
My personal consciousness is my voice.
Help me always make the right choice.

My free will seems to have escaped me,
and my genes decide without asking me.
So come, Risen Jesus, friend of the birds.

I will be your disciple to the end.
Daily transformed by your kindness,
I will be kind to all of your little ones.

(This sonnet is shaped by the tender teachings of
Jesus, the in-depth psychology of Carl Jung, and
code breaking genetic research).

Glossary of Types of Poems in this Book

Acrostic: a poem in which the first letter in each line forms a word or words.

Free style poetry: Popular among poets today. Free style poetry, not tied to rhythm and cadence, frees the poet to express his/her own thoughts. See **Nature's Darkness**, pages. 44-46.

Haiku: A Japanese formatted poem that has three lines. The first and third lines have 5 syllables, and the second line has seven syllables. The emphasis is on brevity, and the syllable count may vary slightly. Nature is usually the subject. However, the subject is not limited to nature.
The third line is usually a surprise or ah ha moment.

Haibun: A poem that starts with a prose statement and ends with a haiku.

Limerick: A limerick is a five-line poem that consists of a single stanza, an AABBA rhyme scheme, and whose subject is a short, tale or description. Most limericks are comedic.

Photo poems, see p. 52.

Sand dab: A sand dab is a short poem named after the sand dab fish. It is often just one line, like this one by Mary Oliver— "Are the morning kisses the sweetest?"

Sijo: A Korean style of lyrical poetry originally called "short song." Sijo resembles Japanese haiku in having a foundation in nature, but neither sijo nor haiku are limited to nature as subject. Like haiku, Sijo has three lines, with 14-16 syllables in each line, for a total of 44-46 syllables. The count may vary slightly as in haiku. In sijo, there is a pause in the middle of each line, so in English they are sometimes printed in six lines instead of three.

Sonnet: A Sonnet is a poem with fourteen lines that uses any of a number of formal rhyme schemes. In English a sonnet typically has ten syllables per line. However, all definitions of poetry must be taken with a grain of salt. Historically, the poet has been granted freedom to alter syllable count, rhyme, and rhythm without reason. Free style poetry is popular today.

Tanka: A haiku with two additional lines of seven syllables each. Syllable count may vary slightly.

Steller's Jay Sonnet

Here I stand an old man and child,
at communion rail with candles lit.
Remembering Jesus meek and mild,
who asked the children to come and sit.

A heart bird came and sat on the rail.
Took a sunflower heart seed from dish.
Called to my consciousness the holy grail,
and Jesus sharing loaves of bread and fish.

Honors with love each communion guest. Says,
God cares for birds and flowers.
God cares for you and me, and all the rest.

A flash of blue came as a swaying band.
A Steller's jay lights softly in my hand.
Let us feed hungry children of the world.

I am amazed at
this Steller's jay's antics.
Blue fire lit in nature.
A blaze of wild gyration.
Magical beauty streaming.

No ticket needed
Nature's not a place to visit
It's home every day

Let's open our hearts
In compassion to each other
Let kindness blossom

In the heart bird's eyes
We see radiance of all things
An epiphany

BOOKS BY DWAYNE COLE

(My wife, Beth, is a professional editor,
and made major contributions to these books)

A Center that Holds: Adventures in Kindness
Alpenglow Miracles: Fire Dance of Wonder
A Prayer of Blessing: As You Go Remember This
A Relational Hermeneutic of Kindness
A Relational Trinity of Kindness
BEARS AND MOOSE OF ALASKA: Nature Poetry
Black-Capped Chickadees: Messengers of Good News
Clouds of Inspiration
Down on the Farm in Georgia: A Poetic Memoir
Dragonfly Magic
Gentle Galilean Glories: The Tender Teachings of Jesus
God and Evil: An Ode to Kindness
Heart Haiku: Alaska Inspired Photos and Poems
Heart Sijo: Alaska Inspired Photos and Poems
*Jesus' Transforming Beatitudes: Selected Sermons from
    Year A*
Jesus' Transforming Love: Selected Sermons from Year B
*Jesus' Transforming Gentle Teachings: Selected Sermons
    from Year C*
Kindness Is Every Step
Lone Leaf Dancing
Poems Inspired by Process Philosophy
Poet of the Universe: A Vision of Beauty and Goodness.
Rainbows of Hope
Snowshoe Hare Beauty
Steller's Jay Blue Sway
The Apostles' Creed: A Living Creed for the Living Church.
The Bible: A Poetic Journey
*The Book of Revelation: Jesus' Kindness Transforms
    Suffering*
The Serenity Prayer: A Pathway to Peace and Happiness